THE LEGACY OF THE ANCIENT WORLD

EUROPE AND THE AMERICAS

02619

MACDONALD YOUNG BOOKS

First published in 1995 by Macdonald Young Books
Campus 400
Maylands Avenue
Hemel Hempstead
Hertfordshire HP2 7EZ
Originally published as part of the title *Pathways,
Timelines of the Ancient World.*

A CIP catalogue for this book is available from the
British Library

ISBN 0 7500 1811 9

Commissioning Editor: Thomas Keegan
Editors: Jill A. Laidlaw, Samantha Armstrong
Designer: Simon Borrough
Picture Researcher: Juliet Duff
Illustrators: Swanston Publishing Ltd., Jonathan Potter, Steve
Roberts, Deborah Kindred (Simon Girling & Associates)
Adrian Barclay, Lee Montgomery (Beehive Illustration)

Text copyright © 1994 Mike Corbishley
Illustrations copyright © 1994 Macdonald Young Books

Printed in Portugal

Cover illustration: Steve Roberts: right. **Deborah Kindred**:
left.

Cover photograph: Ancient Art And Architecture Collection.

Map artwork: Swanston Publishing Ltd.

Picture Acknowledgements
The author and publisher would like to acknowledge, with
thanks, the following photographic sources:

Michael Holford: 12. **The Mansell Collection**: 25. **The
Board of Trinity College, Dublin**: 17. **Werner Forman
Archive**: 15, 21.

CONTENTS

Words in **bold** are explained in the glossary on pages 26–7.

INTRODUCTION

Today it is possible to travel thousands of kilometres by air from one continent to another in just a few hours. The world seems like a small place because images of people from far-off countries are beamed into our front rooms on to our television sets. In ancient times, travel was difficult and slow — many parts of the world would have been far too dangerous for strangers. Even today, people without modern technology, such as jet travel and television, often know little about the lands and the peoples beyond their own countries, or even beyond their own villages.

Despite these difficulties, there were connections between ancient peoples thousands of years ago. *The Legacy of the Ancient World* tells the stories of some of those connections. This book talks about some of the most important peoples of Northern Europe and Central and South America.

NORTHERN EUROPE

The Celts and the Scythians lived in Northern Europe. These Europeans had well-developed trade links with other peoples in their world and they built great stone monuments such as Stonehenge. Many modern-day Europeans can trace their roots back to the people who settled in Europe during the Bronze Age.

THE AMERICAS

The second part of this book is about some of the world's most recent civilizations, the Mayans, Aztecs and Incas. Their story ends with the coming of the Europeans to the 'New World'.

Throughout *The Legacy of the Ancient World* you will find Time Lines (below). The key dates and events listed in the Time Lines will help you to see what is happening at certain points in each civilization's history. You will be able to relate these dates to some of the other things happening elsewhere in the world.

BRONZE-AGE EUROPE

BC

c. 7000 Copper mined in Romania, Hungary, Yugoslavia. Gold also made into ornaments

c. 4000 Knowledge of metalworking passes to other parts of Europe

c. 2300 Bronze working spreads to Europe including Britain and northern France

THE WORLD

BC

c. 8500 First rock art in the Sahara region
First cultivation of wild grasses in Peru

c. 8300 Glaciers retreat in Europe

c. 7000 First crops cultivated in Mexico and in New Guinea

c. 6500 Britain separates from Europe

Dates are given in the usual way — BC and AD. AD is an abbreviation of two **Latin** words *Anno Domini*. Latin was the language used by the Romans. These two words mean "in the year of the lord". This was the system of dating invented by the Christians. Dates are counted from the birth of Jesus Christ. This system of dating is used in most parts of the world today. For example, the first astronauts to step on to the surface of the moon did so on in July AD 1969 — but this date is usually just written as 1969. Dates before the birth of Christ are counted backwards and have the letters BC after them. For example, the Roman general, Julius Caesar, first invaded Britain in 55 BC and then in the following year, 54 BC.

Sometimes we do not know precise dates for something that happened a very long time ago. You will see the letter c. used before dates like these. It is also an abbreviation of a Latin word, *circa*, which means 'about'.

MAKING BRONZE
By about 1200 BC many everyday objects used in Europe were made of bronze — weapons, tools, household utensils and jewellery. Bronze is a metal made of copper and tin. See pages 10–11.

THE MILK DRINKERS
The Scythians were called the 'horse-milkers' and 'milk-eaters' by the Greeks because they made a drink, called koumiss, from the **fermented** milk of female horses.

FIERCE WARRIORS
Celtic warriors were fierce. Some made themselves look frightening by painting patterns on their bodies and spiking their hair. They carried shields and fought with swords and spears, from fast-moving chariots drawn by horses. See page 16.

FROM GERMANY TO THE MEDITERRANEAN
The defended Celtic settlement of Heuneburg in southern Germany was the stronghold of a noble family who lived here around 400 BC. The style of the defences (they are like Greek strongholds) and the range of **imported** goods (wine, fine pottery and jewellery) from the Mediterranean that have been found here show that the family had many contacts with other countries. See page 17.

North Atlantic Ocean

North Sea

Fossum

SCANDANAVI

BRITISH ISLES

GERMANY

Stonehenge & Maiden Castle

Carnac

FRANCE

Wasserburg

Heuneb

Adriatic Sea

Rome

SPAIN

Mediterranean Sea

MAIDEN CASTLE
The Celtic peoples of northern Europe built defended towns to live in. Maiden Castle's huge banks and ditches — the distance from the bottom of a ditch to the top of a bank is 14 metres! — must have put off many invading enemies. See page 17.

WEAPONS AND A WAGON
We know a lot about the Scythians from the tombs of their rich nobles. The wooden walls of burial chambers were brightly painted and a great number of everyday objects and weapons were placed in tombs. See page 14.

WASSERBURG

One of the defended settlements of the peoples of Bronze-Age Europe was discovered in southern Germany in the Federsee Lake. It is called Wasserburg. Around 1200 BC the settlement was made up of about 40 houses which were strongly defended by wooden walls and gates.
See page 11.

THOUSANDS OF STONES

*In many parts of north-western Europe, circles and lines of stones were put up for **rituals** or religious ceremonies. One of the most impressive stone sites is the row of stones at Carnac in Brittany, France. Thousands of stones stretch in parallel lines across the landscape.*
See page 11.

PART 1:
NORTHERN EUROPE

This part of the book covers the years from about 7000 BC to the occupation of north-western Europe by the Romans in the first century BC. This was a period of prehistory for most of the people of Europe — this means that people did not use writing. It was an important time in the history of northern and central Europe because various peoples came together to form tribes, nations and countries.

STONEHENGE

Of the 900 stone circles that exist in Britain, Stonehenge is the most famous. It was probably constructed as a sort of temple for ceremonies and religious rituals.
See pages 12–13.

SCYTHIAN TERRITORY

MOVING HUGE STONES

The builders of Stonehenge must have been clever to get the huge stones (some weighing 50 tonnes) into position.
See pages 12–13.

Black Sea

Amber Trade Routes
Boundary of Celtic Heartland

GREECE

Aegean Sea

Mycenae ○

THE WANDERING SCYTHIANS

*The Greek historian **Herodotus** wrote about the Scythians. He tells us that they were 'people who take their dwellings with them. Their homes are their waggons'. These waggons contained all the family's possessions and travelled about eight kilometres a day behind their herds of cattle, sheep and horses.*
See pages 14–15.

SCYTHIAN WARRIORS

*The Scythians were a warlike **nomadic** people who lived to the north of the Black and Caspian Seas. Scythian nobles rode horses into battle which were beautifully covered with reins and saddles made of brightly-coloured leather and felt.*
See page 14.

BRONZE-AGE EUROPE

BC
- c. 7000 Copper mined in Romania, Hungary, Yugoslavia. Gold also made into ornaments
- c. 4000 Knowledge of metalworking passes to other parts of Europe
- c. 2300 Bronze working spreads to Europe including Britain and northern France
- c. 2000 Increasing number of fortified settlements in eastern and central Europe
- c. 1250 New weapons and armour made of bronze
- c. 1200 Most everyday objects made of bronze
- c. 700 Iron in common use

Hunting and farming peoples needed a good supply of strong materials to make tools and weapons. At first stone, especially flint, was used. But by about 6000 BC people had discovered that copper ore (see opposite page) could be worked into different shapes. Stone tools did not disappear overnight but metal tools gradually replaced them — bronze at first, followed later by iron. The peoples of the Bronze Age (c. 4000 BC) in Europe began to claim land and build settlements. Some were simple villages, but in central and eastern Europe they began to build **fortified** settlements. People became more warlike, perhaps because they wanted to defend their farming land — and the strongest warriors were the rulers.

ARMOUR

By 1250 BC a Bronze-Age warrior would have carried a bronze sword, **mace** and spear. He would have been armed with a bronze helmet, chest and back plates and leg protectors (below).

MINING

By about 1200 BC everyday objects in Europe were made of bronze. Bronze is a mixture of copper and tin. Here you can see a cross-section of a copper mine. A shaft was dug to reach the copper which was then taken out with picks made from deers' antlers.

THE WORLD

BC

c. 7000 First crops cultivated in Mexico
First cultivation of root crops in New Guinea

c. 6000 First farming villages in China

c. 3500 First civilization based on cities in Sumeria

THEIR LEGACIES

As the controlling chieftains of Bronze-Age Europe became richer a new class of people emerged — the warrior class. We do not know the names of individuals or peoples because this was still a period of prehistory. But we do know that different tribes, or nations, can be identified from the remains of their settlements and burials. During this period boundaries began to be set between peoples and their lands.

c. 1700 New palaces built on Minoan Crete

1339 Pharaoh Tutankhamun of Egypt is buried

c. 1200 Olmec civilization begins in Mesoamerica

776 First Olympic Games held in Greece

753 Traditional date for the founding of Rome

WASSERBURG

In what is now called the Federsee Lake in Germany is an island called Wasserburg (below right). Around 1200 BC it was a small village of about 40 wooden houses. The villagers kept cattle, sheep, pigs, goats and horses. They hunted wild boar, **elk**, bear and deer and fished for pike and catfish.

FOSSUM

In southern Scandinavia there were settlements similar to others in Europe. This rock engraving (above) from Fossum in Sweden shows two warriors on a ship.

CARNAC

The most impressive stone monuments in Europe can be found at Carnac in north-western France (above). Each group of stones is made up of between 10 and 13 parallel rows stretching for several kilometres and consisting of nearly 3,000 upright stones.

SMELTING

The metal needed to make tools and weapons comes from ores — parts of rocks which contain metal. To extract the metal, the ore is heated in a furnace (above). This is called smelting.

During the Bronze Age fragments of ore were laid over wood and then a fire was lit. The melted copper then ran out in the groove you can see here as molten (liquid) metal. It was then reheated with tin and poured into stone moulds.

A bronze incense burner stand from Cyprus.

TRADE

We know that there was a lot of contact between the peoples of Bronze-Age Europe. Tools, weapons and armour of the same type have been found in many different countries. **Archaeologists** have also discovered objects made of materials which can only be found in far-off countries. For example, **amber**, which comes from around the **Baltic Sea** has been found in **Mycenae**. An enormous amount of copper was mined in Austria and **exported** all over Europe. Tin from Cornwall, France, Spain and northern Italy were also traded widely.

STONEHENGE

BC
- c. 3000 First phase of the circular ditch with four stones inside
- c. 2100 80 bluestones brought to make a double circle, never completed
- c. 2000 Huge sarsen stones brought to make the outer circle and a central horseshoe shape

- c. 1550 Bluestones rearranged into horseshoe shape in the centre and a circle. Two circles of holes dug outside the sarsen ring
- c. 1100 The avenue which approaches Stonehenge was extended

There are over 900 stone circles in Britain alone and Stonehenge (right) is probably the most famous stone circle in the world. The farming community which built it in about 3000 BC must have been very rich in order to spare so many people for its construction. The community must also have been well organized. Like most other stone circles the site itself was very carefully measured out. We think that Stonehenge was built as some sort of temple for ceremonies and religious rituals. Some experts believe that Stonehenge was built to make observations of the planets and stars. Careful placing of the stones, perhaps after a year of observation, would have given farmers a sort of calendar. Calculations would tell them when the seasons, and the ceremonies which went with them, were due to be held.

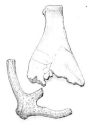

CONSTRUCTION TOOLS

This pickaxe is made from a deer's antler and this shovel was an ox's shoulder blade. The hammer stones pounded the stones into shape.

HOW STONEHENGE WAS BUILT

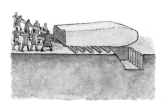

1
The huge stones were moved on wooden rollers to holes which had already been dug with bone and antler tools.

2
The far side of the hole was protected by timbers to stop it breaking down as the stone was levered into place.

3
The stone could then be hoisted up and pushed upright with wooden poles into its foundation hole.

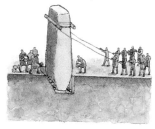

4
The hole was filled in with used hammer stones and chalk which was packed down hard.

BC
c. 3000 First evidence of
hieroglyphic writing
Dingo (dog) introduced into
Australia
c. 2500 City-states in Sumeria
First large settlements in the
Andes region
c. 1900 Indus Valley Civilization in
decline

THEIR ACHIEVEMENTS

Archaeologists working on stone circles have discovered that most of them were very carefully measured. Their builders obviously knew how to measure. But did they use standard measurements, as we do today? Some experts believe they did and one engineer, Professor Alexander Thom, suggested that they were built with a standard measurement of 0.829 metres. However, this measurement does not apply to all the circles in Britain, Ireland and other parts of Europe.

c. 1700 New palaces built on Crete
1339 Pharaoh Tutankhamun
buried
c. 1200 First civilizations in
Mesoamerica
c. 1000 Phoenician alphabet
introduced
Kingdom of Israel ruled by
King David

The stones which form Stonehenge's great arches weigh 50 tonnes and are called sarsen stones. They were brought from 30 kilometres away.

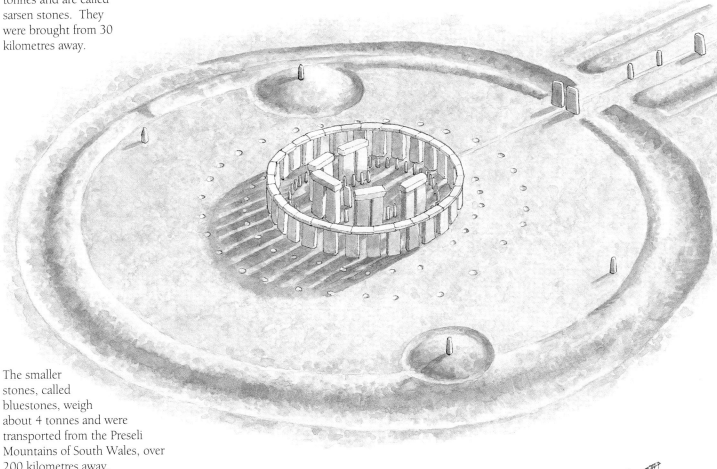

The smaller stones, called bluestones, weigh about 4 tonnes and were transported from the Preseli Mountains of South Wales, over 200 kilometres away.

5

The outer ring of stones was made from two upright stones with a stone laid across the top (called a lintel).

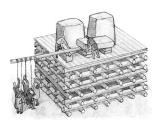

6

The heavy lintel was slowly rolled into position and gradually raised on top of huge timbers.

7

Levers were used to raise the stone at each end so that other timbers could be put underneath it.

8

Finally, the lintel reached the top and could be levered into position across the two upright stones.

13

THE SCYTHIANS

The Scythians were a nomadic people who probably originally came from Central Europe (modern-day Armenia, Russia and the Balkans) in the eighth century BC. They **migrated** south and occupied the land around the Black Sea and the Caspian Sea. Whole groups travelled with their possessions in felt-covered waggons in search of land to graze their cattle, sheep and horses. In the western part of Scythian territory there were some heavily-fortified permanent settlements. The Scythians were a warlike people whose warriors rode horses (like the one below) into battle. We know about the Scythians because of their contact with the Greeks. The Greek historian, Herodotus, wrote that they were fierce warriors whose women... *'...take part in war and wear the same clothes as men. They have a marriage law which forbids a girl to marry until she has killed an enemy in battle'.*

This is a drawing of a horse that was sacrificed and buried with its owner. The horse is wearing a **ceremonial** harness, tailpiece and saddle.

BURIAL TOMBS

Most of the information we have about what the Scythians looked like and the things they used comes from burial chambers which have been **excavated**. Tombs, like the one below from Pazyryk in the Altai Mountains of Siberia, were rooms constructed with large painted timbers. This fifth century BC burial chamber contained a fine waggon which had been dismantled. Other tombs contained slaughtered horses and servants. Above the burial chamber a great mound was built from soil and grass cut from high-quality **pasture** land.

BC
- c. 750 Greek colonies in the Mediterranean
- c. 500 Cast iron first used in China for farm tools and weapons
- c. 400 Olmec civilization in decline
- 327– Alexander the Great
- 325 campaigns in India
- 146 Greece made into Roman provinces
- c. 100 North Vietnam ruled as a Chinese province

THEIR ACHIEVEMENTS

Herodotus described the Scythians as, 'people who take their dwellings with them and are without exception the best archers on horseback. They do not farm but breed animals. Their homes are their waggons.' The Scythians survived until the third century AD *when they were wiped out by invading* **Ostrogoths**.

AD
- c. 100 Kingdom of Axum in Ethiopia established Paper first used in China
- c. 150 Rise of the city of Teotihuacán in the Valley of Mexico

TRADE

The **Greek Empire** lay on the western edge of Scythian territory. Later, these same lands were conquered by the Romans. We know that the Greeks and Scythians traded with each other. Scythian nobles became very rich by selling huge quantities of corn to the Greeks. In return they bought luxury goods, such as drinking cups and bowls, dishes, buckets and *amphorae* (storage jars) full of wine. The Scythians also traded with the Far East. Chinese silk has been found in some Scythian tombs — perhaps the Scythians acted as **agents** for goods brought from the Far East before they were passed on to the peoples of the Mediterranean and western Europe.

ART

The Scythians were fond of brightly-coloured clothes and beautiful objects. This comb (above) is made of gold and shows the Scythians in battle. The warrior on horseback has wounded his opponent's horse (on the right) and another man on the left is entering the fight. This comb was found in the tomb of a rich man and would probably have been a decorative comb used to hold his long hair together.

There was decoration everywhere in Scythian society. Their tents were lined with hangings and there were decorative cushions and carpets on the floor. One carpet, measuring 1.8 metres by 2 metres, was made by the hand-knotting technique — one and a quarter of a million knots were tied to make complicated patterns and pictures of horses, warriors and elks. The bronze cauldrons they cooked in were often decorated with battle scenes or with pictures of animals.

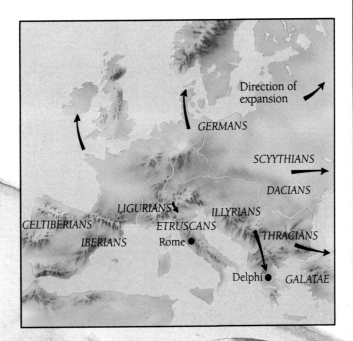

Direction of expansion

GERMANS

SCYYTHIANS

DACIANS

LIGURIANS

CELTIBERIANS

IBERIANS

ETRUSCANS

ILLYRIANS

Rome ●

THRACIANS

Delphi ● GALATAE

This is a Scythian wine jug. It shows Scythian warriors taming wild horses for use in battle.

TATTOOING

The Scythian tombs at Pazyryk in the Altai Mountains have been very well preserved because they have been protected by a layer of ice since about 400 BC. Even the skins of the human bodies were preserved and showed that some people were tattooed. Herodotus wrote that, *'the Scythians consider that tattooing is a mark of noble birth'*. The man drawn above was found in a burial at Pazyryk. He probably died in battle — his body has three battle-axe wounds. The enemy had already cut off his head — the Scythians scalped their enemies and used part of the skull as a drinking bowl. Most of his body had been tattooed with pictures of animals and fish.

THE CELTS

The Celts lived in western Europe from about 700 BC. We know quite a lot about them from their remains and from the ancient Greeks and Romans who wrote about them. Various ancient writers tell us that they were an excitable people. The Greek writer **Strabo** said that Celtic warriors were '*mad keen on war, full of spirit and quick to begin a fight*'. Another historian, called Diodorus Siculus, described Celtic fashion, '*They wear striking clothing, tunics dyed and embroidered in many colours and trousers called* bracae. *They wear striped cloaks, fastened with a brooch, thick in winter and light in summer, in a* **variegated**, *close-set check pattern.*'

The Celts moved across Europe in search of new lands to conquer. They invaded Italy in the fifth century BC and even raided Rome, the capital of the **Roman Empire**, in 390 BC. But they were not just gangs of invading warriors. In the west of Europe they lived in defended hilltop settlements, in villages and on isolated farms. They farmed the land, grew a great variety of crops and kept animals.

The back of a Celtic mirror.

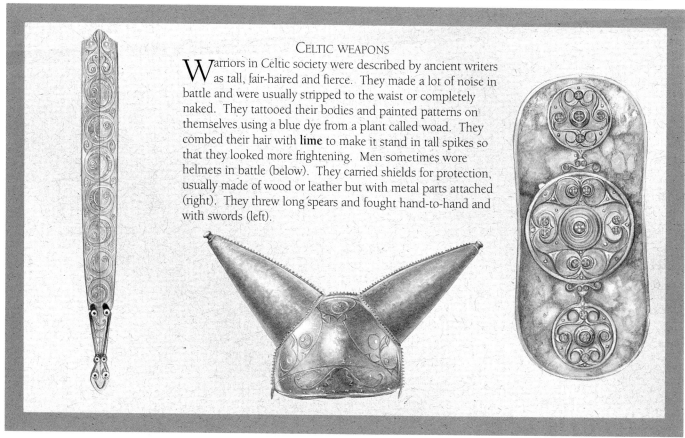

CELTIC WEAPONS

Warriors in Celtic society were described by ancient writers as tall, fair-haired and fierce. They made a lot of noise in battle and were usually stripped to the waist or completely naked. They tattooed their bodies and painted patterns on themselves using a blue dye from a plant called woad. They combed their hair with **lime** to make it stand in tall spikes so that they looked more frightening. Men sometimes wore helmets in battle (below). They carried shields for protection, usually made of wood or leather but with metal parts attached (right). They threw long spears and fought hand-to-hand and with swords (left).

THEIR LEGACIES

Even after the Romans conquered western Europe in the first century BC and drove the Celtic peoples further west, Celtic traditions survived. Traces of Celtic tradition can be found today in several languages which survived the Roman occupation — Breton in Brittany in northern France, Cornish in Cornwall, Welsh in Wales and Gaelic in parts of Scotland and Ireland.

MAIDEN CASTLE

This Celtic town (above) was defended by huge banks, ditches, wooden fences and strong gates.

HEUNEBURG

Heuneburg (above) in modern-day Germany was the home and court of a noble Celtic prince who imported fine Greek and **Etruscan** objects.

Artists carved human heads which give us a good idea of what people looked like (below). Their long, flowing moustaches, said one ancient writer, *'become mixed with food and act as a sort of strainer for the drink to pass through'.*

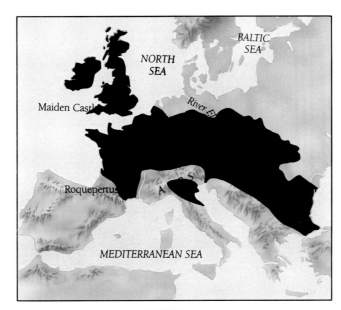

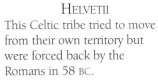

HELVETII

This Celtic tribe tried to move from their own territory but were forced back by the Romans in 58 BC.

RELIGION

The Celts cut off their enemies' heads and placed them in a column at the front of a shrine at Roquepertuse (above).

Celtic art survived long after Britain was freed from the Romans. This is a decorated page from the *Book of Kells* (below) made in Christian Ireland in the early ninth century AD. Compare this decoration with other Celtic objects on these pages.

CELTIC ART

We know that Celtic clothes were bright and colourful but skilled craftspeople also made a number of highly-decorated objects. Favourite or important possessions, such as mirrors and weapons, must have taken great skill to make. Most decorated Celtic objects were made of metals such as bronze, iron, gold and silver. Really precious objects, such as torcs (neckbands) were made of solid gold (above). Many other objects were decorated in Celtic times apart from weapons — brooches, hairpins, rings, horse harness fittings and horse armour, for example. Metal was decorated in different ways — either incised (scratched) on the surface or hammered in. Some metal objects were coloured with paints for extra decoration. Although many objects were just decorated with patterns, Celtic people also liked objects with animal designs on them. Horses were often used to decorate coins but other animals such as cats, wild boar, dogs, birds, rams and cows also appear.

THE GIANT JAGUAR TEMPLE
Worship of the gods was very important for the Mayan people. They built huge stone temples in the form of pyramids. Look at page 20 to find the temple of the Giant Jaguar at Tikal in modern-day Guatemala.

WRITING WITH GLYPHS
*Mayan writing was **hieroglyphic**. **Inscriptions** were carved outside temples and other public buildings. The longest Mayan inscription ever found has 2,500 glyphs and is in the city of Copán. Glyphs are often found on carvings and paintings giving the names of people. See page 20.*

PART 2: THE AMERICAS

The first Americans hunted and gathered their food but by 7000 BC crops were being grown in Mexico. Advanced civilizations grew up in **Mesoamerica** — the Mayans, the Incas and the Aztecs. It was thousands of years before Europeans reached this continent. The first were the Vikings around AD 1000 who sailed to North America. From 1494 onwards the Spaniards and Portuguese arrived and divided the 'New World' between themselves.

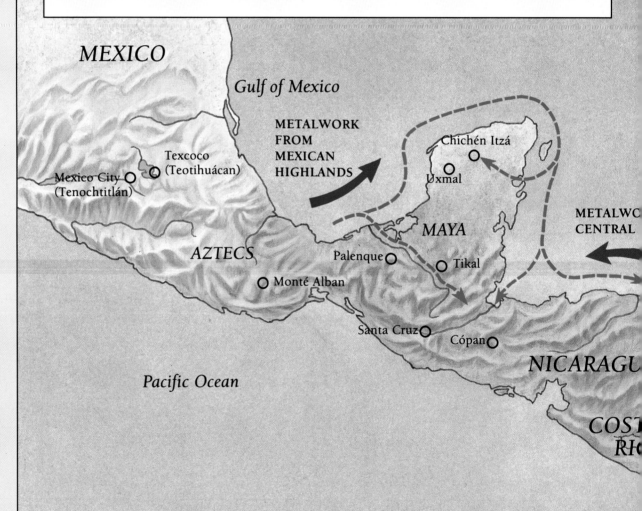

MEXICO

Gulf of Mexico

METALWORK FROM MEXICAN HIGHLANDS

Chichén Itzá

Texcoco (Teotihuácan)

Uxmal

Mexico City (Tenochtitlán)

MAYA

METALWO CENTRAL

AZTECS

Palenque

Monté Alban

Tikal

Santa Cruz

Cópan

Pacific Ocean

NICARAGU

COST RIC

AN EAGLE AND A SNAKE
The capital city of the Aztec Empire was called Tenochtitlán, which means the 'Place of the Prickly Pear Cactus' in Quechua (the Aztec language). The name came from an incident in 1325 when the Aztecs were migrating to find a new home. An omen was seen — an eagle perched on the top of a cactus holding a snake — which told them where to found their city. See page 25.

HUMAN SACRIFICE
The Aztecs believed that the gods had sacrificed themselves as 'food' for the sun and the moon. They believed that human blood had to be offered to the gods to stop the world from coming to an end. See page 25.

18

COUNTING AND SEEING INTO THE FUTURE
The Mayans had two complicated ways of measuring time. Their calendar began about 3114 BC by our system of measuring time. One calendar calculated days and months. The other calendar could only be understood by priests and was used to avoid doing things on days which were supposed to bring bad luck. See page 21.

BRILLIANT ASTRONOMERS
The Mayans built large cities. At Copán, in the modern-day country of Honduras priests watched the stars and the planets and were able to calculate the length of the month almost as accurately as astronomers do today.

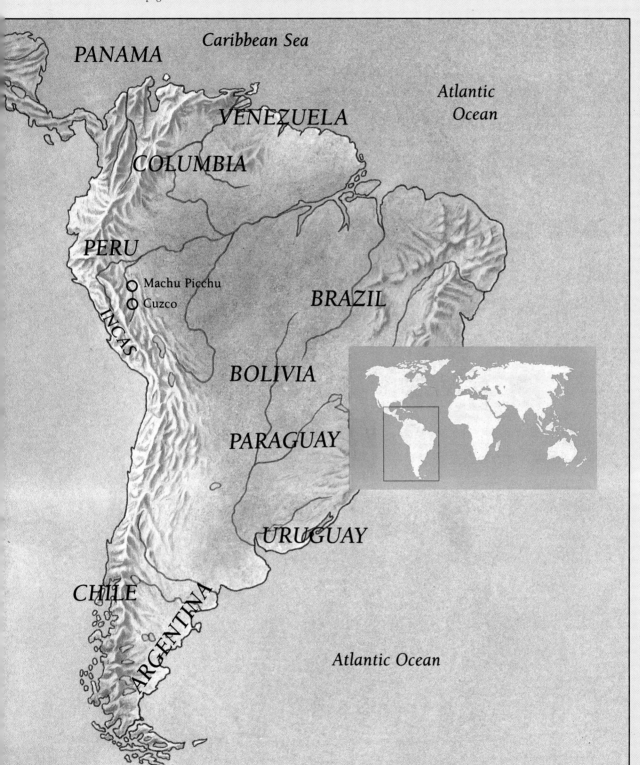

Caribbean Sea

PANAMA

VENEZUELA

Atlantic Ocean

COLUMBIA

PERU

INCAS

○ Machu Picchu

○ Cuzco

BRAZIL

BOLIVIA

PARAGUAY

URUGUAY

CHILE

ARGENTINA

Atlantic Ocean

INCA ROADS
The Incas built thousands of kilometres of roads across their empire to control their people and trade. Inca engineers were very clever at constructing bridges across deep gorges. There were no wheeled vehicles but the llama was used as a pack-animal. See page 23.

BUILDING WITH STONE
*Machu Picchu is one of the most impressive sites of the ancient world. About 1,000 Inca people lived there, high in the mountains. Large blocks of hard granite were skilfully cut by **masons** to construct house and terrace walls. No mortar (cement) was used to hold the blocks in place and they were cut so that they fitted together perfectly. See pages 22 and 23.*

AZTEC TEMPLES
*Religion, and the rituals and ceremonies that went with it, were an important part of Aztec life. Large pyramid temples, called teocalli, were built inside **sacred** courtyards surrounded by a wall. There would also be other public and sacred buildings in the courtyard such as ball courts, racks to hold human skulls and temple schools. See page 24.*

CUZCO, THE INCA CAPITAL
The Incas told the story that their capital city, Cuzco, had been founded by their first emperor, Manco Capac. Cuzco was the centre of the Inca Empire. The empire's 'four quarters', as they were called, radiated out from Cuzco's central plaza. Remains of many of Cuzco's buildings survive despite the destruction of the city by Spanish invaders in 1533. See pages 22–3.

THE MAYANS

BC

c. 2000 First Mayan peoples settle

c. 300– Mayan people influenced by Olmec
AD

c. 300 civilization Ceremonial centres built at places like Tikal

c. 300– Golden age of Mayan

c. 800 civilization Great cities built

615 Pacal becomes ruler of Palenque when 12

683 Pacal dies

c. 800 Lowland Mayan cities abandoned Civilization in decline

c. 980 Toltecs invade Mayan territory. Mayan civilization continues under Toltec rule

1200 Chichén Itzá abandoned

1328 Mayapan becomes the capital

1517– Spanish conquest of
41 Guatemala and Yucatán

For 600 years the Mayan civilization flourished in the part of the Americas we now call Mesoamerica or central America — the land which links north and south America. Mayan territory lies in the modern-day countries of Gautemala, Belize and Mexico. Mayan civilization reached its height around AD 300 when there were many large cities and religious centres with enormous public buildings. Mayan cities were all separate states with their own rulers. They were constantly at war with each other to capture their enemies to sacrifice to the gods.

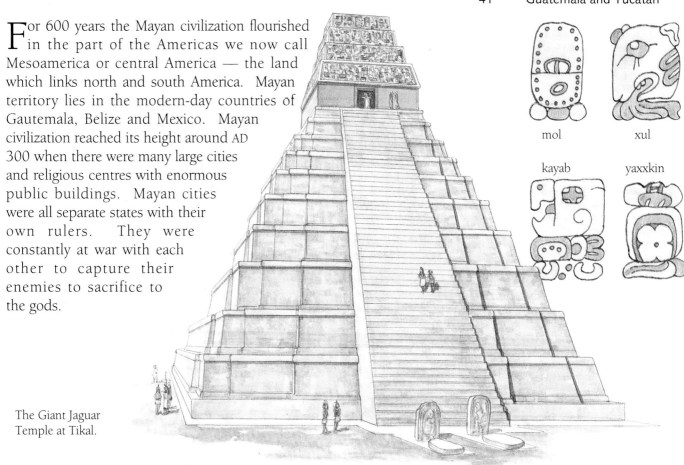

The Giant Jaguar Temple at Tikal.

mol   xul

kayab   yaxxkin

AGRICULTURE

Producing food was very important as there were as many as 50,000 people living in some Mayan cities. Mayan farmers grew a great variety of crops — **maize**, chilli peppers, squash and beans. To increase the amount of food they could grow, Mayan farmers developed a special **irrigation** system of small raised fields on the edges of swamps and rivers (left).

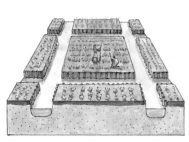

WRITING

The Mayas used a hieroglyphic system of writing (right). A series of 'glyphs' or pictures, gave the names of objects, rulers and cities. Glyphs were often carved or painted on stone. Four books, written on tree-bark paper have been found. We think that ancient Mayan writing may be similar to the language spoken by some Mayan people today.

tzec   muan

mac   kankin

THE WORLD

BC
c. 2000 Minoan civilization on Crete
334 Alexander the Great invades Persian Empire
c. 100 Celts develop defended settlements
AD
79 Roman cities of Pompeii and Herculaneum destroyed by the volcano Vesuvius
c. 100 First use of paper in China

THEIR LEGACIES

The Mayans produced one of the most important civilizations in the Americas. They probably learned from an earlier civilization, the Olmecs, who lived just to the north of them. But unlike the Olmecs, the Mayans perfected writing and complex calendars. The earliest dated writing in the Americas comes from the early Mayan period. The Mayans are also famous for being the first people to construct huge stone-built cities.

300 Yamato state in Japan controls the whole country
475 Romulus Augustulus the last Roman Emperor in the West
c. 1000 Viking settlements in Labrador and Newfoundland
1202 Arab numerals introduced into Europe
1341 Black Death begins in Asia

MAYAN SCULPTURE

Mayan artists modelled stone, **jade** and clay. This figure (above) is from the burial island of Jaina, off the north coast of Mayan lands. Figures were made of gods, rulers and warriors.

RELIGION

Many religious beliefs were shared by the different peoples of the Americas. The Mayans worshipped a number of gods and built huge temples in their honour. They called the god who created their universe Itzam Na. There were gods of the sun and the moon, rain gods called *chaacs*, and individual gods for important aspects of Mayan life.

A sacred pyramid and statue in Chichén Itzá.

CHICHÉN ITZÁ

At the city of Chichén Itzá the Mayans built a round tower, 24 metres tall to watch the movements of the stars.

PALENQUE

In AD 615 a new ruler, called Pacal, took control of the city of Palenque. During Pacal's reign the city became the centre of a large state.

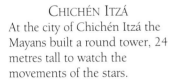

Gulf of Mexico • Chichén Itzá
Mayapan •
Tikal ▲
Palenque •
• Copán
Pacific Ocean

TIKAL

By the eighth century AD the city of Tikal had a population of around 50,000 people. There were five temple pyramids which were built on top of the tombs of past rulers of the city.

TWO CALENDARS

The Mayans had two calendars for calculating time. One was 365 days long and the other, a religious calendar, was made up of 260 days divided into 13 weeks of 20 days each. This sacred calendar was used to predict the future. The two wheels on the right show how the sacred calendar worked — the wheel on the left shows the 13 weeks, the one on the right the glyphs (or names) for each of the 20 days.

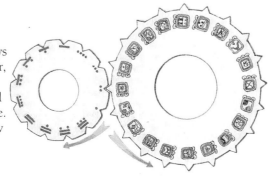

BALL COURTS

The centre of Mayan cities were large squares, or plazas, surrounded by huge buildings such as temple pyramids, palaces, great ceremonial causeways and ball courts. A ceremonial ballgame, called *tlachti*, was played all over Mesoamerica. The game was like modern basketball with two teams. But it was a rough game — players were often injured or killed.

THE INCAS

The Incas grew from a small tribe, around AD 1200, into an enormous empire of eight million people along the Andes mountain range of South America (in modern-day Ecuador, Peru, Bolivia and Chile). According to Inca legend their first ruler, Manco Capac, founded the capital at Cuzco. The Inca leader was known as *Sapa Inca*, which means 'the only emperor'. In the fifteenth century AD Emperor Pachacuti extended Inca territory both north and south and by the next century the Inca Empire stretched from (modern-day) Ecuador to (modern-day) Chile. A large Inca army conquered new lands and kept people under control. Hostile peoples were forced to move into places in Inca territory where they could be supervised. The Incas called their empire *Tahuantinsuyu* which meant the 'Land of the Four Quarters'. The emperor appointed a governor to rule each quarter. Most Incas were farmers. They grew a wide range of food — from maize to beans, chilli peppers, potatoes, avocados and peanuts. People also ate pigs and ducks.

The Inca town of Machu Picchu.

THE INCA COUNTING SYSTEM
The Incas did not use writing but they did keep historical records. The *quipucamayoc* were state-appointed accountants who kept records on knotted cords, called *quipu*. These were cords of different colours with single, double or treble knots tied in them to mark events and accounts.

22

AD
- c. 1200 Rise of the Kingdom of Mali in west Africa
- 1241 Swedes now rule Finland
- 1309 Popular crusades launched in Europe
- c. 1350 Maori people on North Islands of New Zealand
- 1381 Peasants' revolt in England

THEIR LEGACIES

Every person throughout the Inca Empire had to do some work for the state each year. It was known as mit'a and could involve labouring in the mines or on the roads or serving in the army. The invasion of the Spaniards (during the 1530s) put an end to the Inca Empire. But some parts of the ancient Inca civilization have survived. Most of the Indians who live in the Andes today still speak Quechua (the original Inca language) and those who look after herds still count them using the quipu.

- 1456 Ottoman Turks capture Athens
- 1497 Portuguese Vasco da Gama sails to India via the Cape of Good Hope
- 1516 Coffee is first imported into Europe

INCA ROADS

The Incas needed roads to control their empire. They were excellent engineers who built over 23,000 kilometres of roads. Government runners provided a 24-hour service carrying messages between relay stations (called *tambos*) about 2.5 kilometres apart.

Roads (above) were built in straight lines where possible but they sometimes had to zig-zag up and down steep mountains.

Inca engineers had to continue roads across rivers and streams. They built **suspension bridges** made out of twisted plant **fibres**.

TRANSPORT

There were no wheeled vehicles anywhere in the Americas before the arrival of Europeans. Important officials, like the empire's governors, were carried on **litters**. In the Inca Empire goods were carried on peoples' backs or on animals such as llamas (above).

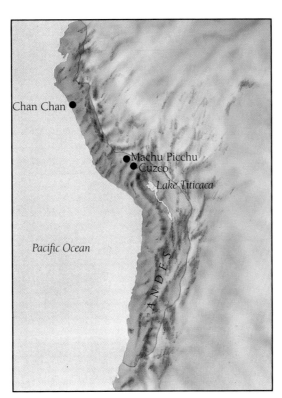

Chan Chan

Machu Picchu
Cuzco

Lake Titicaca

Pacific Ocean

ANDES

CUZCO

Modern-day Cuzco is built on top of the Inca capital planned by the Emperor Pachacuti in 1438.

CHAN CHAN

The Chimú people lived on the desert coast of northern Peru. Chan Chan was their capital. They were eventually conquered by the Incas.

MACHU PICCHU

This fortress city was built on a rock ridge surrounded by mountains. The land on each side of the city was terraced into fields. About 1,000 people lived in one-roomed houses grouped around open courtyards. Granite stone was cut into irregular shapes for walls and buildings.

RELIGION

The Incas worshipped their own ancestors. **Mummified** bodies were taken out of their tombs to attend ceremonies. The most important of these ancestors were the emperors. The Incas believed that the emperor was a direct descendant of the sun god, called Inti. The Incas also worshipped Wiraqocha, the creator, Killa, the moon goddess, Illapa, the god of thunder, Pachamama, the earth goddess and Mamaqocha, god of the sea. Temples were built throughout the empire for the worship of the gods. The most important was in the capital city, Cuzco. The temple was called Qorikancha, the 'Temple of the Sun'. Ceremonies for the gods usually involved sacrifice of animals, such as llamas or guinea pigs, and offerings of food or cloth but, sometimes, humans were also sacrificed.

THE AZTECS

AD
c. 1300	Aztecs first arrive in the Valley of Mexico
1345	First settlement built on Lake Texcoco
1428	Aztecs control Valley of Mexico after forming the Triple Alliance between Texcoco, Tlacopán and Tenochtitlán
1440–68	Emperor Montezuma I expands the empire to the Gulf of Mexico
1502	Aztec Empire now stretches from the Gulf of Mexico to the Pacific Ocean
1519	Spanish invaders, led by Hernán Cortés, land in Mexico
1520–21	Emperor Montezuma II taken prisoner and killed. All Aztec resistance crushed and civilization destroyed

Aztec legend tells how they, the 'people of Aztlan' to the north-west, were ordered by their god, Huitzilopochtli, to migrate to new lands in about AD 1300. Eventually they settled on the shores of Lake Texcoco in the Valley of Mexico. Here they built their capital, Tenochtitlán (below). The Aztecs were very warlike. They fought endless battles with neighbouring peoples until they became the most powerful group in the area. By 1428 they controlled the whole of the Valley of Mexico. Around 1500 they were in charge of a huge empire of ten million people. The supreme ruler of the Aztecs was the emperor, called *Tlatoani*, meaning 'Speaker' in Quechua. The emperor was elected by the royal family, the priests and the most important warriors. The empire was very rich. Captured luxury goods, such as cloth, and other resources, such as gold, silver and precious stones, were carried by merchants into the cities of the empire. Around 60,000 people came to trade in Tenochtitlán every day.

RELIGION AND WAR

Most Aztec boys, but especially from the nobility, went to military schools from the age of ten. Some boys and girls went to religious schools but only the boys went on to become priests. Religion was an important part of everyones' lives. Hundreds of gods and goddesses were believed to be responsible for what happened to people, the land, the skies and the sea. Huge temples, like these at Tenochtitlán (below), were built to the gods. Human sacrifice was an essential part of these ceremonies. Wars were fought mainly to capture people to sacrifice to the gods.

WRITING

Most Aztec writing used pictograms — pictures which represented words (above). Pictograms were painted on paper made from the inner bark of the fig tree, or on animal skins or cotton cloth. This writing recorded taxes, religious ceremonies, histories, maps and plans.

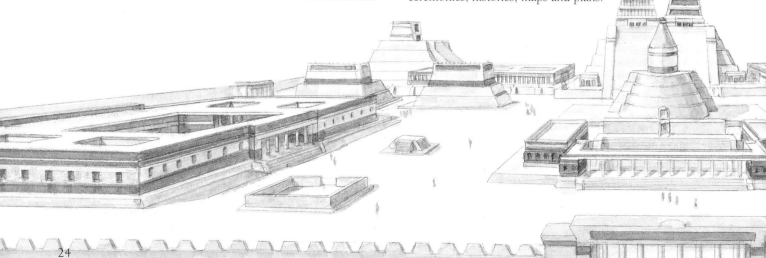

AD

c. 1300	Rise of the kingdom of Benin in Nigeria
1350	Firearms first used in Europe
1368	Ming Dynasty founded in China
1381	Peasants' Revolt in England
1421	Capital of China moved to Beijing (Peking)
1453	Constantinople falls to the Ottoman Turks
1492	Columbus sails to the Bahamas from Europe

THEIR LEGACIES

When the Spanish invaders reached Mexico in 1519 they found a very advanced civilization. Although the Europeans were horrified at the human sacrifices in Aztec temples, they came to cities which were much larger than anything in Spain at the time. The Spaniards destroyed the Aztec Empire and imposed Christianity, a European way of life and the Spanish language on the country.

1492	Granada, the last Muslim stronghold in Spain, is reconquered by the Christians
1497	Portuguese Vasco da Gama sails to India around Africa
1520	Reign of Suleiman the Magnificent, the golden age of the Muslim Ottoman Empire
	Chocolate is first imported into Europe

THE VALLEY OF MEXICO

Aztec people were divided into two classes — the *pipiltin*, or nobles, and the *macehualtin*, the ordinary people. Most ordinary people were farmers, who either worked their own land or the land owned by noble families. There were also the *tlacotin*, who were slaves owned by the nobles. The Valley of Mexico had excellent farming land but Aztec farmers also created 'floating islands' of heaped-up mud. The most important crops were maize, squash, sweet potato, avocado and tomato.

TENOCHTITLÁN

The ruins of the capital city of the Aztec Empire, which was home to over 200,000 people, lie under the modern-day capital, Mexico City. The city was carefully laid out on a grid of streets and canals built over swampy land. The huge city was connected to the mainland by three wide highways.

Gulf of Mexico

Tenochtitlan

Pacific Ocean

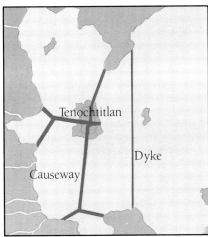

Tenochtitlan

Dyke

Causeway

INVASION FROM EUROPE

The history of the Americas changed when Europeans crossed the Atlantic Ocean and discovered new lands. The people who lived there must have regretted that they had been 'discovered' at all. Native Americans, north and south, were killed in huge numbers and were infected with diseases from Europe, such as **smallpox** and measles, against which they had no **immunity**. Invading armies were followed by new governors and merchants who transported back to the 'Old World' huge supplies of gold and silver. The Europeans also brought back plants and animals which are now familiar European foods — such as potatoes, marrows, peppers and turkeys.

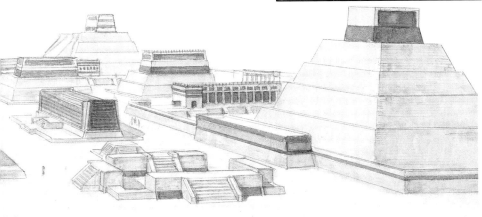

GLOSSARY

A

agents: people who conduct business on behalf of others. For example, a merchant might sell his goods to an agent, and then the agent will sell the goods to another merchant, who will in turn sell them to his or her customers.

amber: a fossil that comes from certain types of extinct trees. Amber is a beautiful yellowish-brown colour and is often used in jewellery-making.

archaeologist: someone who studies the past by scientifically examining the remains of the past. Archaeologists often **excavate** objects in their search for knowledge.

B

Baltic Sea: the sea near countries such as Poland, Denmark, Finland and Norway.

C

ceremonial: anything, such as food or clothing, that is connected with a ceremony. Ceremonies are often related to religions and traditions.

E

elk: a large deer that lives in North America, northern Europe and Asia. In North America an elk is called a moose.

Etruscan: the name of ancient people who originally lived north of Rome from about 900 BC onwards. The Etruscans were very wealthy. Their riches came from farming, trade, metalworking and pottery-making. The Etruscans eventually controlled an empire which stretched from Mantua to the Bay of Naples.

excavate: to find and dig up an item from the past.

Bones, objects, and entire buildings have been excavated.

export: to sell and transport goods to another country

F

fermented: a chemical reaction in a food or drink usually caused by yeast. This chemical reaction turns sugar into alcohol.

fibre: a very thin thread of material or plant which can be spun or twisted with other fibres to make cloth, rope or a structure.

fortified: a house, town or city which is defended by either walls, watchtowers, ditches or a moat.

G

Greek Empire: the trading and colonial empire established by the Greek civilizations. The Minoans established the first Greek Empire about 4,000 years ago. The Myceneans then became the most powerful people in Greece around 1500 BC. Around 1200 BC Classical Greek culture became dominant and around 700 BC the Greek city-states ran the empire.

H

Herodotus: (c. 484–424) a Greek historian who wrote about many aspects of Greek life including nine books about the war between the Greeks and the Persians from 490–449 BC.

hieroglyphic: words that are represented by pictures and symbols.

I

immunity: human beings have immunity to certain illnesses, such as the common cold. This means that our bodies can resist disease and recover from illness.

import: to buy and transport goods produced in another country.

inscriptions: words, pictures or symbols carved into rock, bone, stone or wood.

irrigation: to water farm land by a system of small canals or ditches which carry water to the fields from a source such as a river.

J
jade: a semiprecious stone used in jewellery-making. Jade can be white or green in colour.

L
Latin: the language of ancient Rome and the Roman Empire. Latin was used as the language of learning in medieval Europe. Books such as the Old and New *Testaments* of the *Bible* were written in Latin. Latin is no longer spoken anywhere so it is called a 'dead' language.

lime: a mineral found in certain types of clay.

litter: a form of transport consisting of a chair or a small bed fixed to two poles or sticks, carried from place to place.

M
mace: a weapon, rather like a club, usually held as a symbol of authority.

maize: a grain crop from Latin America which was vital to ancient **Mesoamerican** civilizations. Maize is sometimes called sweetcorn in Europe.

mason: someone who is skilled in building with stone and carving stone for decorative purposes.

Mesoamerica: a name for ancient central America.

migrate: to travel from one place to another in search of a home.

mummified: a body which has been preserved after death has been mummified. Mummification involves drying out the body and then treating it with chemicals to help preserve it.

Mycenae: a hill-top town, defended by strong outer walls that was the capital of the Mycenaean Civilization of ancient Greece. The Mycenaeans were the most powerful people in Greece by about 1500 BC. Mycenae was on the Greek island of Crete.

N

nomadic: people who travel from place to place in search of food for themselves and their cattle.

O
Ostrogoths: the name of the eastern Goths who ruled their own Italian empire.

P
pasture: fields set aside for animals to graze on.

R
ritual: a series of actions usually associated with a religious ceremony.

Roman Empire: the name of the lands ruled by the ancient Romans. At the height of Roman power the empire stretched from west and southern Europe to Africa and southwest Asia. The Empire began to decline after 395 AD.

S
sacred: an object or building that is dedicated to one particular God, an object or place that is thought of as holy because of its connection with a religion or a god.

smallpox: a virus which can be easily passed from person to person (this is called contagious). People with smallpox have a high temperature and fever and become covered with spots. When the spots dry up and fall off the body they leave pits in the skin which never disappear. Smallpox can now be treated with modern medicine but up until very recently many people died from it.

Strabo: (c. 63– c. 23 AD), a Greek historian and geographer who wrote an important book on ancient geography called *Geographica*. Very little is known about Strabo, we are not even sure of when he was born and when he died.

suspension bridge: a bridge where the walking platform is held between two towers by cables of some sort. The cables have to be very strong.

V
variegated: something which has had colours added to it or which has a pattern which gives the impression of constantly changing its appearance.

INDEX